WHAT DO I KNOW ABOUT MY GOD?

A 12 Week Bible Study for Ages 8-12

Kelly Collier

ISBN: 978-1-959592-02-0

Formatting and cover design by Reflecting the Designer
reflectingthedesigner.org

Table of Contents

HOW TO DO THIS STUDY

Do you know why God gave us the Bible? Because God wants us to know Him. He invites us to know Him. And He doesn't make getting to know Him difficult. This is why He gave us the Bible. The Bible is like a personal letter from God. Every page of this letter tells us about our wonderful God—who He is and what He does. And the best part is: you can read this letter for yourself.

This study focuses on one very special part of this letter that God gave us: the book of Psalm. You can easily find this book in your Bible by opening it right in the very middle. With 150 chapters, Psalm is the longest book in the Bible. In each of the weeks to follow, you will be directed to read specially chosen verses from Psalm. "Why Psalm," you may ask? Because this one book contains so many verses that tell us plainly what God is like.

I love to read. And I especially love to read books about real people like George Washington and Queen Elizabeth. These types of books are called biographies. An author researches the life of a famous person and then records the story of that individual in a book. In this study, we will be like the author, researching the life and character of a real person. Only in this case, the Person we want to know about is God. As you follow the simple steps described below, you will create your own journal full of wonderful truths about God. You could call it your own biography of God. But this kind of study is far better than just reading a book or simply learning facts about God. As you get to know God better, you will also grow to love and trust Him more. Knowing God and believing what He says about Himself will change you! (2 Corinthians 3:18)

Before you begin, take time to read through the steps below. As you work on your study in the weeks to come, you may run into something difficult to understand. When this happens, please ask a trusted adult for help. And don't forget to share with them what God is teaching you about Himself. Spiritually, we grow best when we grow with other people!

🙏 STEP 1: PREPARE

Reading the Bible is different from reading any other book in the whole world. That is because the Bible is unlike any other book in the whole world. It is a spiritual book, authored by God Himself. If we work hard and have a good teacher, we can usually figure out a math or science lesson. But getting to know God is different from studying a book from school. Because the Bible is a spiritual book, we won't be able to understand it unless we have God's help—no matter how hard we work at it. That is why you need to prepare your heart before you open your Bible. God also gave us a wonderful Teacher, the Holy Spirit, who helps us understand what we read so we can know our great God. PRAY and ask God to help you understand what you are reading. God loves to answer this humble prayer!

🔍 STEP 2: OBSERVE
Ask: What Do I Know About My God?

After asking God for help, open your Bible to the verses listed for that day. To observe simply means that we *look* for something as we read the Bible. Better yet, we look for SOMEONE as we read. READ through the verses and LOOK for what those verses teach you about God. You may need to read the verses over a second or third time. Don't rush through your reading. Slow down. Be like a skilled detective and ask good questions as you read (like the questions provided below). WRITE DOWN anything you learn about Him.

Here are some ideas of what you can look for as you read:

- **What is God like?** (Look for descriptive words like *good, faithful,* and *powerful*.)
- **What does God do?** (Look for action words like *protects, delivers,* and *loves*.)

Think of the following phrases as you read and try to fill in the blank:

My God is _____ (Example: *My God is merciful.*)

My God _____ (Example: *My God hates sin.*)

⚤ STEP 3: APPLY
Ask: If I Believe This About God, How Will I Live?

Don't stop with simply writing down truths you learn about God. God wants what you are learning about Him to change you. To apply simply means that we take time to think about how truth about God relates to our lives as His children. Think about how a famous chef doesn't just know a lot of facts about cooking but is also able to put that knowledge into action. Knowledge applied results in food that tastes really good! In a similar way, God wants us to take the knowledge about Him that we get from the Bible and put it to work in our everyday lives. It is dangerous for us to learn facts about God without allowing God to change us. What is the danger? Scripture warns that we will become proud (1 Cor. 8:1). How can you guard your heart from pride? By prayerfully applying God's Word to your life. Remember, it is not enough to **hear** what God says; we must also **do** what God says. Check out James 1:22: *"But be doers of the word, and not hearers only, deceiving yourselves."* We lie to ourselves if we think we know God but aren't doing what He says. So, every time you read the Bible you should ask this question: What does God want me to do?

Seeing God's amazing character should humble us. And because we know that God loves us, we don't have to fear being honest with Him about the ways we need to change and grow. He wants us to know Him. And He wants us to become more like Him.

Take time to THINK about what you learned about God and WRITE DOWN anything you need to do with God's help.

Here are some questions you could ask yourself:

- If I really **believe** this truth about God, then how will I live?
- Do I need to **ask God's forgiveness** for a way I have been
- thinking or acting against His character?
- How can I **act** on this truth about God in my everyday life?
- How can I **show other people** this truth about my God?

 **STEP 4: PRAY**

We cannot trust or obey God in our own strength. We need God! So just as you started your time in God's Word by talking to Him, end your time in God's Word by talking to Him. Praise Him for His amazing character. Thank Him for what He does for you. Ask Him for the strength you need to trust and obey Him. WRITE OUT your prayer to God.

Thank God for what you learned about Him.

> *God, thank you that you are* _____ .

Ask God for His help to obey.

> *God, today I learned that You don't want me to be afraid. Every time I am tempted to fear, please help me to think about You and to trust You.*

EXTRA TREASURE: Scripture Memory

Do you know someone who can watch a movie one time and quote all the funny lines from memory? Maybe you are like that. Kids have amazing memories! God gave us minds that can remember all kinds of things. He wants us to use this gift to remember the most important thing: His Word. In fact, God's Word is so precious, He tells us we should not just remember it, but store it up like a treasure in our hearts (Psalm 119:11). You treasure God's Word by reading it, thinking about it, and memorizing it so you can remember it and put it into practice all day long. You will find a special passage for you to memorize at the start of each week's study. You can commit to treasuring God's Word just like the author of Psalm 119:16.

> *I will delight in your statutes; I will not forget your word.*
> (Psalm 119:16)

WHAT DO I KNOW ABOUT MY GOD?

Weekly Study Pages

WEEK ONE

Psalm 8:1

*O LORD, our Lord, how majestic is your name in all the earth!
You have set your glory above the heavens.*

Monday | God is my... My God is...

🙏 PREPARE: Getting my heart ready to meet with God.

We need God's help to understand His Word. Begin your time in the Word today by thoughtfully praying these words of Scripture back to the Lord:

Give me understanding, that I may keep your law and observe it with my whole heart. (Psalm 119:34)

🔍 OBSERVE: Getting God's Word into my heart.

Read **Psalm 3:1-8** and seek to answer the question: *What do these verses teach me about My God?*

_____

_____

_____

_____

_____

❓ APPLY: Getting God's Word into my life.

Think about what you learned about God. Ask: *If I really believe this truth about God, then how will I live?*

_____

_____

_____

_____

_____

🙏 MY PRAYER TO GOD: Thank God for what you learned about Him. Ask God for His help to obey.

_____

_____

_____

_____

Tuesday | God is my... My God is...

PREPARE: Getting my heart ready to meet with God.

We need God's help to understand His Word. Begin your time in the Word today by thoughtfully praying these words of Scripture back to the Lord:

> *Open my eyes, that I may behold wondrous things*
> *out of your law. (Psalm 119:18)*

OBSERVE: Getting God's Word into my heart.

Read **Psalm 5:1-6, 11-12** and seek to answer the question: *What do these verses teach me about My God?*

_____

_____

_____

_____

_____

APPLY: Getting God's Word into my life.

Think about what you learned about God. Ask: *If I really believe this truth about God, then how will I live?*

_____

_____

_____

_____

MY PRAYER TO GOD: Thank God for what you learned about Him. Ask God for His help to obey.

_____

_____

_____

_____

Wednesday | God is my... My God is...

PREPARE: Getting my heart ready to meet with God.

We need God's help to understand His Word. Begin your time in the Word today by thoughtfully praying these words of Scripture back to the Lord:

> *You have said, "Seek my face." My heart says to you, "Your face, LORD, do I seek." (Psalm 27:8)*

OBSERVE: Getting God's Word into my heart.
Read **Psalm 8:1-9** and seek to answer the question: *What do these verses teach me about My God?*

_____

_____

_____

_____

APPLY: Getting God's Word into my life.
Think about what you learned about God. Ask: *If I really believe this truth about God, then how will I live?*

_____

_____

_____

_____

MY PRAYER TO GOD: Thank God for what you learned about Him. Ask God for His help to obey.

_____

_____

_____

_____

Thursday | God is my... My God is...

PREPARE: Getting my heart ready to meet with God.

We need God's help to understand His Word. Begin your time in the Word today by thoughtfully praying these words of Scripture back to the Lord:

Make me to know your ways, O LORD; teach me your paths. Lead me in your truth and teach me, for you are the God of my salvation... (Psalm 25:4-5)

OBSERVE: Getting God's Word into my heart.

Read **Psalm 9:1-10** and seek to answer the question: *What do these verses teach me about My God?*

_____

_____

_____

_____

_____

APPLY: Getting God's Word into my life.

Think about what you learned about God. Ask: *If I really believe this truth about God, then how will I live?*

_____

_____

_____

_____

MY PRAYER TO GOD: Thank God for what you learned about Him. Ask God for His help to obey.

_____

_____

_____

_____

Friday | God is my... My God is...

PREPARE: Getting my heart ready to meet with God.

We need God's help to understand His Word. Begin your time in the Word today by thoughtfully praying these words of Scripture back to the Lord:

Teach me to do your will, for you are my God!
(Psalm 143:10a)

OBSERVE: Getting God's Word into my heart.
Read **Psalm 16:1-11** and seek to answer the question: *What do these verses teach me about My God?*

_____

_____

_____

_____

APPLY: Getting God's Word into my life.
Think about what you learned about God. Ask: *If I really believe this truth about God, then how will I live?*

_____

_____

_____

_____

MY PRAYER TO GOD: Thank God for what you learned about Him. Ask God for His help to obey.

_____

_____

_____

_____

Saturday | "Take Five" Weekly Review

Use the journal pages you filled out earlier this week to help
you answer the questions below.

1. Use the space below to write out one of your favorite verses
   from your study this week. Why was this verse special to
   you?

   _____

   _____

   _____

   _____

   _____

   _____

2. What was your favorite truth about God that you learned
   this week?

   _____

   _____

   _____

   _____

   _____

   _____

3. How can you use what you learned about God this week to
   encourage someone else? *(Who will you tell about your great
   God? What will you tell them about Him?)*

   _____

   _____

   _____

   _____

   _____

   _____

4. What is one thing God taught you this past week that you want to change in order to be more like Him? Stop and ask God to give you the grace to obey!

_____

_____

_____

_____

_____

_____

5. How did "what you know about God" help you this past week? *(Think about a difficulty you faced or a decision you had to make where remembering the truth about God helped you do the right thing.)*

_____

_____

_____

_____

_____

_____

Psalm 8:1

O LORD, our Lord, how majestic is your name in all the earth!
You have set your glory above the heavens.

Sunday | Worship

You should worship God every day. But Sunday is a special day set aside in our week to really focus on giving worship to our great God. Use this sheet to help prepare your heart to worship the Lord at church today. Begin your "worship service" at home, praising God for who He is and what He has done for you.

God created you to worship Him.

Worthy are you, our Lord and God, to receive glory and honor and power, for you created all things, and by your will they existed and were created. (Revelation 4:11)

God is worthy of your worship.

Worthy is the Lamb who was slain, to receive power and wealth and wisdom and might and honor and glory and blessing! (Revelation 5:12)

The Psalm are all about our great God! Each chapter is full of incredible truths about God. Look back through this week's journal pages and write down at least 5 things you learned about our amazing God: "Who He is" or "What He does." Then take time to praise God, through prayer, for each thing you wrote down. You might even want to grab a hymnal and sing a song of praise to God.

I will praise Him for **Who He is**	*I will praise Him for* **What He does**
1. My God is: _____	1. My God does: _____
2. My God is: _____	2. My God does: _____
3. My God is: _____	3. My God does: _____
4. My God is: _____	4. My God does: _____
5. My God is: _____	5. My God does: _____

WEEK TWO

Psalm 18:1-2

I love you, O LORD, my strength.
The LORD is my rock and my fortress and my deliverer,
my God, my rock, in whom I take refuge, my shield,
and the horn of my salvation, my stronghold.

Monday | God is my... My God is...

🙏 PREPARE: Getting my heart ready to meet with God.

We need God's help to understand His Word. Begin your time in the Word today by thoughtfully praying these words of Scripture back to the Lord:

Give me understanding, that I may keep your law and observe it with my whole heart. (Psalm 119:34)

🔍 OBSERVE: Getting God's Word into my heart.

Read **Psalm 18:1-6** and seek to answer the question: *What do these verses teach me about My God?*

_____

_____

_____

_____

_____

❓ APPLY: Getting God's Word into my life.

Think about what you learned about God. Ask: *If I really believe this truth about God, then how will I live?*

_____

_____

_____

_____

🙏 MY PRAYER TO GOD: Thank God for what you learned about Him. Ask God for His help to obey.

_____

_____

_____

_____

Tuesday | God is my... My God is...

PREPARE: Getting my heart ready to meet with God.

We need God's help to understand His Word. Begin your time in the Word today by thoughtfully praying these words of Scripture back to the Lord:

Open my eyes, that I may behold wondrous things out of your law. (Psalm 119:18)

OBSERVE: Getting God's Word into my heart.
Read **Psalm 18:25-32** and seek to answer the question: *What do these verses teach me about My God?*

_____

_____

_____

_____

APPLY: Getting God's Word into my life.
Think about what you learned about God. Ask: *If I really believe this truth about God, then how will I live?*

_____

_____

_____

_____

MY PRAYER TO GOD: Thank God for what you learned about Him. Ask God for His help to obey.

_____

_____

_____

_____

Wednesday | God is my... My God is...

🙏 **PREPARE:** Getting my heart ready to meet with God.

We need God's help to understand His Word. Begin your time in the Word today by thoughtfully praying these words of Scripture back to the Lord:

> *You have said, "Seek my face." My heart says to you,*
> *"Your face, LORD, do I seek." (Psalm 27:8)*

🔍 **OBSERVE:** Getting God's Word into my heart.

Read **Psalm 19:1-14** and seek to answer the question: *What do these verses teach me about My God?*

_____

_____

_____

_____

_____

🎯 **APPLY:** Getting God's Word into my life.

Think about what you learned about God. Ask: *If I really believe this truth about God, then how will I live?*

_____

_____

_____

_____

🙏 **MY PRAYER TO GOD:** Thank God for what you learned about Him. Ask God for His help to obey.

_____

_____

_____

_____

Thursday | God is my... My God is...

PREPARE: Getting my heart ready to meet with God.

We need God's help to understand His Word. Begin your time in the Word today by thoughtfully praying these words of Scripture back to the Lord:

Make me to know your ways, O LORD; teach me your paths. Lead me in your truth and teach me, for you are the God of my salvation... (Psalm 25:4-5)

OBSERVE: Getting God's Word into my heart.
Read **Psalm 23:1-6** and seek to answer the question: *What do these verses teach me about My God?*

_____

_____

_____

_____

_____

APPLY: Getting God's Word into my life.
Think about what you learned about God. Ask: *If I really believe this truth about God, then how will I live?*

_____

_____

_____

_____

MY PRAYER TO GOD: Thank God for what you learned about Him. Ask God for His help to obey.

_____

_____

_____

_____

Friday | God is my... My God is...

PREPARE: Getting my heart ready to meet with God.

We need God's help to understand His Word. Begin your time in the Word today by thoughtfully praying these words of Scripture back to the Lord:

Teach me to do your will, for you are my God!
(Psalm 143:10a)

OBSERVE: Getting God's Word into my heart.

Read **Psalm 24:1-10** and seek to answer the question: *What do these verses teach me about My God?*

_____

_____

_____

_____

APPLY: Getting God's Word into my life.

Think about what you learned about God. Ask: *If I really believe this truth about God, then how will I live?*

_____

_____

_____

_____

MY PRAYER TO GOD: Thank God for what you learned about Him. Ask God for His help to obey.

_____

_____

_____

_____

Saturday | "Take Five" Weekly Review

Use the journal pages you filled out earlier this week to help you answer the questions below.

1. Use the space below to write out one of your favorite verses from your study this week. Why was this verse special to you?

_____

_____

_____

_____

_____

2. What was your favorite truth about God that you learned this week?

_____

_____

_____

_____

_____

3. How can you use what you learned about God this week to encourage someone else? (Who will you tell about your great God? What will you tell them about Him?)

_____

_____

_____

_____

_____

4. What is one thing God taught you this past week that you want to change in order to be more like Him? Stop and ask God to give you the grace to obey!

_____

_____

_____

_____

_____

5. How did "what you know about God" help you this past week? *(Think about a difficulty you faced or a decision you had to make where remembering the truth about God helped you do the right thing.)*

_____

_____

_____

_____

_____

Psalm 18:1-2

I love you, O LORD, my strength.
The LORD is my rock and my fortress and my deliverer,
my God, my rock, in whom I take refuge, my shield,
and the horn of my salvation, my stronghold.

Sunday | Worship

You should worship God every day. But Sunday is a special day set aside in our week to really focus on giving worship to our great God. Use this sheet to help prepare your heart to worship the Lord at church today. Begin your "worship service" at home, praising God for who He is and what He has done for you.

God created you to worship Him.

Worthy are you, our Lord and God, to receive glory and honor and power, for you created all things, and by your will they existed and were created. (Revelation 4:11)

God is worthy of your worship.

Worthy is the Lamb who was slain, to receive power and wealth and wisdom and might and honor and glory and blessing! (Revelation 5:12)

The Psalm are all about our great God! Each chapter is full of incredible truths about God. Look back through this week's journal pages and write down at least 5 things you learned about our amazing God: "Who He is" or "What He does." Then take time to praise God, through prayer, for each thing you wrote down. You might even want to grab a hymnal and sing a song of praise to God.

I will praise Him for **Who He is**	*I will praise Him for* **What He does**
1. My God is: _____	1. My God does: _____
2. My God is: _____	2. My God does: _____
3. My God is: _____	3. My God does: _____
4. My God is: _____	4. My God does: _____
5. My God is: _____	5. My God does: _____

WEEK THREE

Psalm 27:1

The LORD is my light and my salvation;
whom shall I fear? The LORD is the stronghold of my life;
of whom shall I be afraid?

Monday | God is my... My God is...

PREPARE: Getting my heart ready to meet with God.

We need God's help to understand His Word. Begin your time in the Word today by thoughtfully praying these words of Scripture back to the Lord:

Give me understanding, that I may keep your law and observe it with my whole heart. (Psalm 119:34)

OBSERVE: Getting God's Word into my heart.
Read **Psalm 25:1-15** and seek to answer the question: *What do these verses teach me about My God?*

_____

_____

_____

_____

_____

APPLY: Getting God's Word into my life.
Think about what you learned about God. Ask: *If I really believe this truth about God, then how will I live?*

_____

_____

_____

_____

_____

MY PRAYER TO GOD: Thank God for what you learned about Him. Ask God for His help to obey.

_____

_____

_____

_____

Tuesday | God is my... My God is...

PREPARE: Getting my heart ready to meet with God.

We need God's help to understand His Word. Begin your time in the Word today by thoughtfully praying these words of Scripture back to the Lord:

> *Open my eyes, that I may behold wondrous things*
> *out of your law. (Psalm 119:18)*

OBSERVE: Getting God's Word into my heart.

Read **Psalm 27:1-14** and seek to answer the question: *What do these verses teach me about My God?*

_____

_____

_____

_____

_____

APPLY: Getting God's Word into my life.

Think about what you learned about God. Ask: *If I really believe this truth about God, then how will I live?*

_____

_____

_____

_____

_____

MY PRAYER TO GOD: Thank God for what you learned about Him. Ask God for His help to obey.

_____

_____

_____

_____

Wednesday | God is my... My God is...

PREPARE: Getting my heart ready to meet with God.

We need God's help to understand His Word. Begin your time in the Word today by thoughtfully praying these words of Scripture back to the Lord:

> You have said, "Seek my face." My heart says to you,
> "Your face, LORD, do I seek." (Psalm 27:8)

OBSERVE: Getting God's Word into my heart.
Read **Psalm 28:1-2, 6-9** and seek to answer the question: *What do these verses teach me about My God?*

_____

_____

_____

_____

_____

APPLY: Getting God's Word into my life.
Think about what you learned about God. Ask: *If I really believe this truth about God, then how will I live?*

_____

_____

_____

_____

MY PRAYER TO GOD: Thank God for what you learned about Him. Ask God for His help to obey.

_____

_____

_____

_____

Thursday | God is my... My God is...

PREPARE: Getting my heart ready to meet with God.

We need God's help to understand His Word. Begin your time in the Word today by thoughtfully praying these words of Scripture back to the Lord:

Make me to know your ways, O LORD; teach me your paths. Lead me in your truth and teach me, for you are the God of my salvation... (Psalm 25:4-5)

OBSERVE: Getting God's Word into my heart.

Read **Psalm 30:1-12** and seek to answer the question: *What do these verses teach me about My God?*

_____

_____

_____

_____

_____

APPLY: Getting God's Word into my life.

Think about what you learned about God. Ask: *If I really believe this truth about God, then how will I live?*

_____

_____

_____

_____

MY PRAYER TO GOD: Thank God for what you learned about Him. Ask God for His help to obey.

_____

_____

_____

_____

Friday | God is my... My God is...

🙏 PREPARE: Getting my heart ready to meet with God.

We need God's help to understand His Word. Begin your time in the Word today by thoughtfully praying these words of Scripture back to the Lord:

Teach me to do your will, for you are my God!
(Psalm 143:10a)

🔍 OBSERVE: Getting God's Word into my heart.
Read **Psalm 31:1-8, 14-16, 19-20** and seek to answer the question: *What do these verses teach me about My God?*

_____

_____

_____

_____

_____

🔱 APPLY: Getting God's Word into my life.
Think about what you learned about God. Ask: *If I really believe this truth about God, then how will I live?*

_____

_____

_____

_____

_____

🙏 MY PRAYER TO GOD: Thank God for what you learned about Him. Ask God for His help to obey.

_____

_____

_____

_____

Saturday | "Take Five" Weekly Review

Use the journal pages you filled out earlier this week to help you answer the questions below.

1. Use the space below to write out one of your favorite verses from your study this week. Why was this verse special to you?

_____

_____

_____

_____

_____

_____

2. What was your favorite truth about God that you learned this week?

_____

_____

_____

_____

_____

_____

3. How can you use what you learned about God this week to encourage someone else? *(Who will you tell about your great God? What will you tell them about Him?)*

_____

_____

_____

_____

_____

4. What is one thing God taught you this past week that you want to change in order to be more like Him? Stop and ask God to give you the grace to obey!

_____

_____

_____

_____

_____

_____

5. How did "what you know about God" help you this past week? *(Think about a difficulty you faced or a decision you had to make where remembering the truth about God helped you do the right thing.)*

_____

_____

_____

_____

_____

_____

Psalm 27:1

The LORD is my light and my salvation;
whom shall I fear? The LORD is the stronghold of my life;
of whom shall I be afraid?

Sunday | Worship

You should worship God every day. But Sunday is a special day set aside in our week to really focus on giving worship to our great God. Use this sheet to help prepare your heart to worship the Lord at church today. Begin your "worship service" at home, praising God for who He is and what He has done for you.

God created you to worship Him.

Worthy are you, our Lord and God, to receive glory and honor and power, for you created all things, and by your will they existed and were created. (Revelation 4:11)

God is worthy of your worship.

Worthy is the Lamb who was slain, to receive power and wealth and wisdom and might and honor and glory and blessing! (Revelation 5:12)

The Psalm are all about our great God! Each chapter is full of incredible truths about God. Look back through this week's journal pages and write down at least 5 things you learned about our amazing God: "Who He is" or "What He does." Then take time to praise God, through prayer, for each thing you wrote down. You might even want to grab a hymnal and sing a song of praise to God.

I will praise Him for **Who He is**	*I will praise Him for* **What He does**
1. My God is: _____	1. My God does: _____
2. My God is: _____	2. My God does: _____
3. My God is: _____	3. My God does: _____
4. My God is: _____	4. My God does: _____
5. My God is: _____	5. My God does: _____

WEEK FOUR

Psalm 34:8

Oh, taste and see that the LORD is good!
Blessed is the man who takes refuge in him!

Monday | God is my... My God is...

🙏 PREPARE: Getting my heart ready to meet with God.

We need God's help to understand His Word. Begin your time in the Word today by thoughtfully praying these words of Scripture back to the Lord:

Give me understanding, that I may keep your law and observe it with my whole heart. (Psalm 119:34)

🔍 OBSERVE: Getting God's Word into my heart.

Read **Psalm 32:1-11** and seek to answer the question: *What do these verses teach me about My God?*

_____

_____

_____

_____

_____

❓ APPLY: Getting God's Word into my life.

Think about what you learned about God. Ask: *If I really believe this truth about God, then how will I live?*

_____

_____

_____

_____

_____

🙏 MY PRAYER TO GOD: Thank God for what you learned about Him. Ask God for His help to obey.

_____

_____

_____

_____

Tuesday | God is my... My God is...

PREPARE: Getting my heart ready to meet with God.

We need God's help to understand His Word. Begin your time in the Word today by thoughtfully praying these words of Scripture back to the Lord:

> *Open my eyes, that I may behold wondrous things out of your law. (Psalm 119:18)*

OBSERVE: Getting God's Word into my heart.

Read **Psalm 33:1-9** and seek to answer the question: *What do these verses teach me about My God?*

_____

_____

_____

_____

_____

APPLY: Getting God's Word into my life.

Think about what you learned about God. Ask: *If I really believe this truth about God, then how will I live?*

_____

_____

_____

_____

MY PRAYER TO GOD: Thank God for what you learned about Him. Ask God for His help to obey.

_____

_____

_____

_____

Wednesday | God is my... My God is...

🙏 PREPARE: Getting my heart ready to meet with God.

We need God's help to understand His Word. Begin your time in the Word today by thoughtfully praying these words of Scripture back to the Lord:

> *You have said, "Seek my face." My heart says to you,*
> *"Your face, LORD, do I seek." (Psalm 27:8)*

🔍 OBSERVE: Getting God's Word into my heart.

Read **Psalm 33:10-22** and seek to answer the question: *What do these verses teach me about My God?*

_____

_____

_____

_____

❔ APPLY: Getting God's Word into my life.

Think about what you learned about God. Ask: *If I really believe this truth about God, then how will I live?*

_____

_____

_____

_____

🙏 MY PRAYER TO GOD: Thank God for what you learned about Him. Ask God for His help to obey.

_____

_____

_____

Thursday | God is my... My God is...

PREPARE: Getting my heart ready to meet with God.

We need God's help to understand His Word. Begin your time in the Word today by thoughtfully praying these words of Scripture back to the Lord:

Make me to know your ways, O LORD; teach me your paths.
Lead me in your truth and teach me, for you are the God of my
salvation... (Psalm 25:4-5)

OBSERVE: Getting God's Word into my heart.

Read **Psalm 34:1-10** and seek to answer the question: *What do these verses teach me about My God?*

_____

_____

_____

_____

_____

APPLY: Getting God's Word into my life.

Think about what you learned about God. Ask: *If I really believe this truth about God, then how will I live?*

_____

_____

_____

_____

MY PRAYER TO GOD: Thank God for what you learned about Him. Ask God for His help to obey.

_____

_____

_____

_____

Friday | God is my... My God is...

🙏 PREPARE: Getting my heart ready to meet with God.

We need God's help to understand His Word. Begin your time in the Word today by thoughtfully praying these words of Scripture back to the Lord:

Teach me to do your will, for you are my God!
(Psalm 143:10a)

🔍 OBSERVE: Getting God's Word into my heart.
Read **Psalm 34:15-22** and seek to answer the question: *What do these verses teach me about My God?*

_____

_____

_____

_____

_____

❓ APPLY: Getting God's Word into my life.
Think about what you learned about God. Ask: *If I really believe this truth about God, then how will I live?*

_____

_____

_____

_____

_____

🙏 MY PRAYER TO GOD: Thank God for what you learned about Him. Ask God for His help to obey.

_____

_____

_____

_____

Saturday | "Take Five" Weekly Review

Use the journal pages you filled out earlier this week to help you answer the questions below.

1. Use the space below to write out one of your favorite verses from your study this week. Why was this verse special to you?

_____

_____

_____

_____

_____

_____

2. What was your favorite truth about God that you learned this week?

_____

_____

_____

_____

_____

3. How can you use what you learned about God this week to encourage someone else? (*Who will you tell about your great God? What will you tell them about Him?*)

_____

_____

_____

_____

_____

4. What is one thing God taught you this past week that you want to change in order to be more like Him? Stop and ask God to give you the grace to obey!

_____

_____

_____

_____

_____

_____

5. How did "what you know about God" help you this past week? *(Think about a difficulty you faced or a decision you had to make where remembering the truth about God helped you do the right thing.)*

_____

_____

_____

_____

_____

_____

Psalm 34:8

Oh, taste and see that the LORD is good!
Blessed is the man who takes refuge in him!

Sunday | Worship

You should worship God every day. But Sunday is a special day set aside in our week to really focus on giving worship to our great God. Use this sheet to help prepare your heart to worship the Lord at church today. Begin your "worship service" at home, praising God for who He is and what He has done for you.

God created you to worship Him.

Worthy are you, our Lord and God, to receive glory and honor and power, for you created all things, and by your will they existed and were created. (Revelation 4:11)

God is worthy of your worship.

Worthy is the Lamb who was slain, to receive power and wealth and wisdom and might and honor and glory and blessing! (Revelation 5:12)

The Psalm are all about our great God! Each chapter is full of incredible truths about God. Look back through this week's journal pages and write down at least 5 things you learned about our amazing God: "Who He is" or "What He does." Then take time to praise God, through prayer, for each thing you wrote down. You might even want to grab a hymnal and sing a song of praise to God.

I will praise Him for **Who He is**	*I will praise Him for* **What He does**
1. My God is: _____	1. My God does: _____
2. My God is: _____	2. My God does: _____
3. My God is: _____	3. My God does: _____
4. My God is: _____	4. My God does: _____
5. My God is: _____	5. My God does: _____

WEEK FIVE

Psalm 40:16

*But may all who seek you rejoice and be glad in you;
may those who love your salvation say continually,
"Great is the LORD!"*

Monday | God is my... My God is...

PREPARE: Getting my heart ready to meet with God.

We need God's help to understand His Word. Begin your time in the Word today by thoughtfully praying these words of Scripture back to the Lord:

Give me understanding, that I may keep your law and observe it with my whole heart. (Psalm 119:34)

OBSERVE: Getting God's Word into my heart.

Read **Psalm 36:5-12** and seek to answer the question: *What do these verses teach me about My God?*

_____

_____

_____

_____

_____

APPLY: Getting God's Word into my life.

Think about what you learned about God. Ask: *If I really believe this truth about God, then how will I live?*

_____

_____

_____

_____

_____

MY PRAYER TO GOD: Thank God for what you learned about Him. Ask God for His help to obey.

_____

_____

_____

_____

Tuesday | God is my... My God is...

PREPARE: Getting my heart ready to meet with God.

We need God's help to understand His Word. Begin your time in the Word today by thoughtfully praying these words of Scripture back to the Lord:

> *Open my eyes, that I may behold wondrous things out of your law. (Psalm 119:18)*

OBSERVE: Getting God's Word into my heart.
Read **Psalm 37:1-7, 23-24, 39-40** and seek to answer the question: *What do these verses teach me about My God?*

_____

_____

_____

_____

APPLY: Getting God's Word into my life.
Think about what you learned about God. Ask: *If I really believe this truth about God, then how will I live?*

_____

_____

_____

_____

MY PRAYER TO GOD: Thank God for what you learned about Him. Ask God for His help to obey.

_____

_____

_____

_____

Wednesday | God is my... My God is...

PREPARE: Getting my heart ready to meet with God.

We need God's help to understand His Word. Begin your time in the Word today by thoughtfully praying these words of Scripture back to the Lord:

> *You have said, "Seek my face." My heart says to you, "Your face, LORD, do I seek." (Psalm 27:8)*

OBSERVE: Getting God's Word into my heart.
Read **Psalm 40:1-5, 16-17** and seek to answer the question: *What do these verses teach me about My God?*

_____

_____

_____

_____

APPLY: Getting God's Word into my life.
Think about what you learned about God. Ask: *If I really believe this truth about God, then how will I live?*

_____

_____

_____

_____

MY PRAYER TO GOD: Thank God for what you learned about Him. Ask God for His help to obey.

_____

_____

_____

_____

Thursday | God is my... My God is...

🙏 PREPARE: Getting my heart ready to meet with God.

We need God's help to understand His Word. Begin your time in the Word today by thoughtfully praying these words of Scripture back to the Lord:

Make me to know your ways, O LORD; teach me your paths. Lead me in your truth and teach me, for you are the God of my salvation... (Psalm 25:4-5)

🔍 OBSERVE: Getting God's Word into my heart.

Read **Psalm 46:1-11** and seek to answer the question: *What do these verses teach me about My God?*

_____

_____

_____

_____

_____

🤷 APPLY: Getting God's Word into my life.

Think about what you learned about God. Ask: *If I really believe this truth about God, then how will I live?*

_____

_____

_____

_____

🙏 MY PRAYER TO GOD: Thank God for what you learned about Him. Ask God for His help to obey.

_____

_____

_____

_____

Friday | God is my... My God is...

PREPARE: Getting my heart ready to meet with God.

We need God's help to understand His Word. Begin your time in the Word today by thoughtfully praying these words of Scripture back to the Lord:

Teach me to do your will, for you are my God!
(Psalm 143:10a)

OBSERVE: Getting God's Word into my heart.
Read **Psalm 56:1-13** and seek to answer the question: *What do these verses teach me about My God?*

_____

_____

_____

_____

APPLY: Getting God's Word into my life.
Think about what you learned about God. Ask: *If I really believe this truth about God, then how will I live?*

_____

_____

_____

_____

MY PRAYER TO GOD: Thank God for what you learned about Him. Ask God for His help to obey.

_____

_____

_____

Saturday | "Take Five" Weekly Review

Use the journal pages you filled out earlier this week to help you answer the questions below.

1. Use the space below to write out one of your favorite verses from your study this week. Why was this verse special to you?

_____

_____

_____

_____

_____

_____

2. What was your favorite truth about God that you learned this week?

_____

_____

_____

_____

_____

3. How can you use what you learned about God this week to encourage someone else? *(Who will you tell about your great God? What will you tell them about Him?)*

_____

_____

_____

_____

_____

4. What is one thing God taught you this past week that you want to change in order to be more like Him? Stop and ask God to give you the grace to obey!

_____

_____

_____

_____

_____

5. How did "what you know about God" help you this past week? *(Think about a difficulty you faced or a decision you had to make where remembering the truth about God helped you do the right thing.)*

_____

_____

_____

_____

_____

Psalm 40:16

But may all who seek you rejoice and be glad in you;
may those who love your salvation say continually,
"Great is the LORD!"

Sunday | Worship

You should worship God every day. But Sunday is a special day set aside in our week to really focus on giving worship to our great God. Use this sheet to help prepare your heart to worship the Lord at church today. Begin your "worship service" at home, praising God for who He is and what He has done for you.

God created you to worship Him.

Worthy are you, our Lord and God, to receive glory and honor and power, for you created all things, and by your will they existed and were created. (Revelation 4:11)

God is worthy of your worship.

Worthy is the Lamb who was slain, to receive power and wealth and wisdom and might and honor and glory and blessing! (Revelation 5:12)

The Psalm are all about our great God! Each chapter is full of incredible truths about God. Look back through this week's journal pages and write down at least 5 things you learned about our amazing God: "Who He is" or "What He does." Then take time to praise God, through prayer, for each thing you wrote down. You might even want to grab a hymnal and sing a song of praise to God.

I will praise Him for **Who He is**	*I will praise Him for* **What He does**
1. My God is: _____	1. My God does: _____
2. My God is: _____	2. My God does: _____
3. My God is: _____	3. My God does: _____
4. My God is: _____	4. My God does: _____
5. My God is: _____	5. My God does: _____

WEEK SIX

Psalm 68:19

Blessed be the Lord, who daily bears us up;
God is our salvation.

Monday | God is my... My God is...

🙏 PREPARE: Getting my heart ready to meet with God.

We need God's help to understand His Word. Begin your time in the Word today by thoughtfully praying these words of Scripture back to the Lord:

Give me understanding, that I may keep your law and observe it with my whole heart. (Psalm 119:34)

🔍 OBSERVE: Getting God's Word into my heart.

Read **Psalm 61:1-8** and seek to answer the question: *What do these verses teach me about My God?*

_____

_____

_____

_____

_____

❓ APPLY: Getting God's Word into my life.

Think about what you learned about God. Ask: *If I really believe this truth about God, then how will I live?*

_____

_____

_____

_____

_____

🙏 MY PRAYER TO GOD: Thank God for what you learned about Him. Ask God for His help to obey.

_____

_____

_____

_____

Tuesday | God is my... My God is...

PREPARE: Getting my heart ready to meet with God.

We need God's help to understand His Word. Begin your time in the Word today by thoughtfully praying these words of Scripture back to the Lord:

> *Open my eyes, that I may behold wondrous things out of your law. (Psalm 119:18)*

OBSERVE: Getting God's Word into my heart.
Read **Psalm 62:1-8, 11-12** and seek to answer the question:
What do these verses teach me about My God?

_____

_____

_____

_____

_____

APPLY: Getting God's Word into my life.
Think about what you learned about God. Ask: *If I really believe this truth about God, then how will I live?*

_____

_____

_____

_____

_____

MY PRAYER TO GOD: Thank God for what you learned about Him. Ask God for His help to obey.

_____

_____

_____

_____

Wednesday | **God is my... My God is...**

🙏 PREPARE: Getting my heart ready to meet with God.

We need God's help to understand His Word. Begin your time in the Word today by thoughtfully praying these words of Scripture back to the Lord:

> *You have said, "Seek my face." My heart says to you,*
> *"Your face, LORD, do I seek." (Psalm 27:8)*

🔍 OBSERVE: Getting God's Word into my heart.
Read **Psalm 66:1-7, 16-20** and seek to answer the question: *What do these verses teach me about My God?*

_____

_____

_____

_____

❓ APPLY: Getting God's Word into my life.
Think about what you learned about God. Ask: *If I really believe this truth about God, then how will I live?*

_____

_____

_____

_____

🙏 MY PRAYER TO GOD: Thank God for what you learned about Him. Ask God for His help to obey.

_____

_____

_____

Thursday | God is my... My God is...

🙏 PREPARE: Getting my heart ready to meet with God.

We need God's help to understand His Word. Begin your time in the Word today by thoughtfully praying these words of Scripture back to the Lord:

Make me to know your ways, O LORD; teach me your paths. Lead me in your truth and teach me, for you are the God of my salvation... (Psalm 25:4-5)

🔍 OBSERVE: Getting God's Word into my heart.

Read **Psalm 68:4-6, 19-20, 32-35** and seek to answer the question: *What do these verses teach me about My God?*

_____

_____

_____

_____

_____

🎯 APPLY: Getting God's Word into my life.

Think about what you learned about God. Ask: *If I really believe this truth about God, then how will I live?*

_____

_____

_____

_____

🙏 MY PRAYER TO GOD: Thank God for what you learned about Him. Ask God for His help to obey.

_____

_____

_____

_____

Friday | God is my... My God is...

🙏 PREPARE: Getting my heart ready to meet with God.

We need God's help to understand His Word. Begin your time in the Word today by thoughtfully praying these words of Scripture back to the Lord:

Teach me to do your will, for you are my God!
(Psalm 143:10a)

🔍 OBSERVE: Getting God's Word into my heart.

Read **Psalm 71:1-6** and seek to answer the question: *What do these verses teach me about My God?*

_____

_____

_____

_____

❓ APPLY: Getting God's Word into my life.

Think about what you learned about God. Ask: *If I really believe this truth about God, then how will I live?*

_____

_____

_____

_____

🙏 MY PRAYER TO GOD: Thank God for what you learned about Him. Ask God for His help to obey.

_____

_____

_____

_____

Saturday | "Take Five" Weekly Review

Use the journal pages you filled out earlier this week to help you answer the questions below.

1. Use the space below to write out one of your favorite verses from your study this week. Why was this verse special to you?

_____

_____

_____

_____

_____

_____

2. What was your favorite truth about God that you learned this week?

_____

_____

_____

_____

_____

_____

3. How can you use what you learned about God this week to encourage someone else? *(Who will you tell about your great God? What will you tell them about Him?)*

_____

_____

_____

_____

_____

4. What is one thing God taught you this past week that you want to change in order to be more like Him? Stop and ask God to give you the grace to obey!

_____

_____

_____

_____

_____

_____

5. How did "what you know about God" help you this past week? *(Think about a difficulty you faced or a decision you had to make where remembering the truth about God helped you do the right thing.)*

_____

_____

_____

_____

_____

_____

Psalm 68:19

Blessed be the Lord, who daily bears us up;
God is our salvation.

Sunday | Worship

You should worship God every day. But Sunday is a special day set aside in our week to really focus on giving worship to our great God. Use this sheet to help prepare your heart to worship the Lord at church today. Begin your "worship service" at home, praising God for who He is and what He has done for you.

God created you to worship Him.

Worthy are you, our Lord and God, to receive glory and honor and power, for you created all things, and by your will they existed and were created. (Revelation 4:11)

God is worthy of your worship.

Worthy is the Lamb who was slain, to receive power and wealth and wisdom and might and honor and glory and blessing! (Revelation 5:12)

The Psalm are all about our great God! Each chapter is full of incredible truths about God. Look back through this week's journal pages and write down at least 5 things you learned about our amazing God: "Who He is" or "What He does." Then take time to praise God, through prayer, for each thing you wrote down. You might even want to grab a hymnal and sing a song of praise to God.

I will praise Him for **Who He is**	*I will praise Him for* **What He does**
1. My God is: _____	1. My God does: _____
2. My God is: _____	2. My God does: _____
3. My God is: _____	3. My God does: _____
4. My God is: _____	4. My God does: _____
5. My God is: _____	5. My God does: _____

WEEK SEVEN

Psalm 84:11

For the LORD God is a sun and shield;
the LORD bestows favor and honor. No good thing
does he withhold from those who walk uprightly.

Monday | God is my... My God is...

🙏 PREPARE: Getting my heart ready to meet with God.

We need God's help to understand His Word. Begin your time in the Word today by thoughtfully praying these words of Scripture back to the Lord:

Give me understanding, that I may keep your law and observe it with my whole heart. (Psalm 119:34)

🔍 OBSERVE: Getting God's Word into my heart.

Read **Psalm 73:23-28** and seek to answer the question: *What do these verses teach me about My God?*

_____

_____

_____

_____

_____

❓ APPLY: Getting God's Word into my life.

Think about what you learned about God. Ask: *If I really believe this truth about God, then how will I live?*

_____

_____

_____

_____

_____

🙏 MY PRAYER TO GOD: Thank God for what you learned about Him. Ask God for His help to obey.

_____

_____

_____

_____

Tuesday | God is my... My God is...

⬥ PREPARE: Getting my heart ready to meet with God.

We need God's help to understand His Word. Begin your time in the Word today by thoughtfully praying these words of Scripture back to the Lord:

Open my eyes, that I may behold wondrous things out of your law. (Psalm 119:18)

🔍 OBSERVE: Getting God's Word into my heart.
Read **Psalm 77:11-15** and seek to answer the question: *What do these verses teach me about My God?*

_____

_____

_____

_____

⬥ APPLY: Getting God's Word into my life.
Think about what you learned about God. Ask: *If I really believe this truth about God, then how will I live?*

_____

_____

_____

_____

⬥ MY PRAYER TO GOD: Thank God for what you learned about Him. Ask God for His help to obey.

_____

_____

_____

_____

Wednesday | God is my... My God is...

PREPARE: Getting my heart ready to meet with God.

We need God's help to understand His Word. Begin your time in the Word today by thoughtfully praying these words of Scripture back to the Lord:

> You have said, "Seek my face." My heart says to you,
> "Your face, LORD, do I seek." (Psalm 27:8)

OBSERVE: Getting God's Word into my heart.

Read **Psalm 84:1-12** and seek to answer the question: *What do these verses teach me about My God?*

_____

_____

_____

_____

APPLY: Getting God's Word into my life.

Think about what you learned about God. Ask: *If I really believe this truth about God, then how will I live?*

_____

_____

_____

_____

MY PRAYER TO GOD: Thank God for what you learned about Him. Ask God for His help to obey.

_____

_____

_____

_____

PREPARE: Getting my heart ready to meet with God.

We need God's help to understand His Word. Begin your time in the Word today by thoughtfully praying these words of Scripture back to the Lord:

Make me to know your ways, O LORD; teach me your paths.
Lead me in your truth and teach me, for you are the God of my
salvation... (Psalm 25:4-5)

OBSERVE: Getting God's Word into my heart.

Read **Psalm 86:1-13** and seek to answer the question: *What do these verses teach me about My God?*

_____

_____

_____

_____

APPLY: Getting God's Word into my life.

Think about what you learned about God. Ask: *If I really believe this truth about God, then how will I live?*

_____

_____

_____

MY PRAYER TO GOD: Thank God for what you learned about Him. Ask God for His help to obey.

_____

_____

_____

Friday | God is my... My God is...

🙏 PREPARE: Getting my heart ready to meet with God.

We need God's help to understand His Word. Begin your time in the Word today by thoughtfully praying these words of Scripture back to the Lord:

Teach me to do your will, for you are my God!
(Psalm 143:10a)

🔍 OBSERVE: Getting God's Word into my heart.

Read **Psalm 91:1-8** and seek to answer the question: *What do these verses teach me about My God?*

_____

_____

_____

_____

_____

❓ APPLY: Getting God's Word into my life.

Think about what you learned about God. Ask: *If I really believe this truth about God, then how will I live?*

_____

_____

_____

_____

🙏 MY PRAYER TO GOD: Thank God for what you learned about Him. Ask God for His help to obey.

_____

_____

_____

_____

Saturday | "Take Five" Weekly Review

Use the journal pages you filled out earlier this week to help you answer the questions below.

1. Use the space below to write out one of your favorite verses from your study this week. Why was this verse special to you?

_____

_____

_____

_____

_____

_____

2. What was your favorite truth about God that you learned this week?

_____

_____

_____

_____

_____

_____

3. How can you use what you learned about God this week to encourage someone else? *(Who will you tell about your great God? What will you tell them about Him?)*

_____

_____

_____

_____

_____

4. What is one thing God taught you this past week that you want to change in order to be more like Him? Stop and ask God to give you the grace to obey!

_____

_____

_____

_____

_____

5. How did "what you know about God" help you this past week? *(Think about a difficulty you faced or a decision you had to make where remembering the truth about God helped you do the right thing.)*

_____

_____

_____

_____

_____

Psalm 84:11

For the LORD God is a sun and shield;
the LORD bestows favor and honor. No good thing
does he withhold from those who walk uprightly.

Sunday | Worship

You should worship God every day. But Sunday is a special day set aside in our week to really focus on giving worship to our great God. Use this sheet to help prepare your heart to worship the Lord at church today. Begin your "worship service" at home, praising God for who He is and what He has done for you.

God created you to worship Him.

Worthy are you, our Lord and God, to receive glory and honor and power, for you created all things, and by your will they existed and were created. (Revelation 4:11)

God is worthy of your worship.

Worthy is the Lamb who was slain, to receive power and wealth and wisdom and might and honor and glory and blessing! (Revelation 5:12)

The Psalm are all about our great God! Each chapter is full of incredible truths about God. Look back through this week's journal pages and write down at least 5 things you learned about our amazing God: "Who He is" or "What He does." Then take time to praise God, through prayer, for each thing you wrote down. You might even want to grab a hymnal and sing a song of praise to God.

I will praise Him for **Who He is**	*I will praise Him for* **What He does**
1. My God is: _____	1. My God does: _____
2. My God is: _____	2. My God does: _____
3. My God is: _____	3. My God does: _____
4. My God is: _____	4. My God does: _____
5. My God is: _____	5. My God does: _____

WEEK EIGHT

Psalm 95:6-7

*Oh come, let us worship and bow down;
let us kneel before the LORD, our Maker!
For he is our God, and we are the people of
his pasture, and the sheep of his hand.*

Monday | God is my... My God is...

PREPARE: Getting my heart ready to meet with God.

We need God's help to understand His Word. Begin your time in the Word today by thoughtfully praying these words of Scripture back to the Lord:

Give me understanding, that I may keep your law and observe it with my whole heart. (Psalm 119:34)

OBSERVE: Getting God's Word into my heart.

Read **Psalm 91:9-16** and seek to answer the question: *What do these verses teach me about My God?*

_____

_____

_____

_____

_____

APPLY: Getting God's Word into my life.

Think about what you learned about God. Ask: *If I really believe this truth about God, then how will I live?*

_____

_____

_____

_____

MY PRAYER TO GOD: Thank God for what you learned about Him. Ask God for His help to obey.

_____

_____

_____

_____

Tuesday | God is my... My God is...

PREPARE: Getting my heart ready to meet with God.

We need God's help to understand His Word. Begin your time in the Word today by thoughtfully praying these words of Scripture back to the Lord:

> *Open my eyes, that I may behold wondrous things*
> *out of your law. (Psalm 119:18)*

OBSERVE: Getting God's Word into my heart.

Read **Psalm 93:1-5** and seek to answer the question: *What do these verses teach me about My God?*

_____

_____

_____

_____

APPLY: Getting God's Word into my life.

Think about what you learned about God. Ask: *If I really believe this truth about God, then how will I live?*

_____

_____

_____

_____

MY PRAYER TO GOD: Thank God for what you learned about Him. Ask God for His help to obey.

_____

_____

_____

_____

Wednesday | God is my... My God is...

🙏 PREPARE: Getting my heart ready to meet with God.

We need God's help to understand His Word. Begin your time in the Word today by thoughtfully praying these words of Scripture back to the Lord:

> *You have said, "Seek my face." My heart says to you,*
> *"Your face, LORD, do I seek." (Psalm 27:8)*

🔍 OBSERVE: Getting God's Word into my heart.

Read **Psalm 95:1-11** and seek to answer the question: *What do these verses teach me about My God?*

_____

_____

_____

_____

APPLY: Getting God's Word into my life.

Think about what you learned about God. Ask: *If I really believe this truth about God, then how will I live?*

_____

_____

_____

_____

🙏 MY PRAYER TO GOD: Thank God for what you learned about Him. Ask God for His help to obey.

_____

_____

_____

Thursday | God is my... My God is...

PREPARE: Getting my heart ready to meet with God.

We need God's help to understand His Word. Begin your time in the Word today by thoughtfully praying these words of Scripture back to the Lord:

Make me to know your ways, O LORD; teach me your paths. Lead me in your truth and teach me, for you are the God of my salvation... (Psalm 25:4-5)

OBSERVE: Getting God's Word into my heart.

Read **Psalm 96:1-13** and seek to answer the question: *What do these verses teach me about My God?*

_____

_____

_____

_____

_____

APPLY: Getting God's Word into my life.

Think about what you learned about God. Ask: *If I really believe this truth about God, then how will I live?*

_____

_____

_____

_____

MY PRAYER TO GOD: Thank God for what you learned about Him. Ask God for His help to obey.

_____

_____

_____

_____

Friday | God is my... My God is...

🙏 PREPARE: Getting my heart ready to meet with God.

We need God's help to understand His Word. Begin your time in the Word today by thoughtfully praying these words of Scripture back to the Lord:

Teach me to do your will, for you are my God!
(Psalm 143:10a)

🔍 OBSERVE: Getting God's Word into my heart.

Read **Psalm 98:1-9** and seek to answer the question: *What do these verses teach me about My God?*

_____

_____

_____

_____

🧐 APPLY: Getting God's Word into my life.

Think about what you learned about God. Ask: *If I really believe this truth about God, then how will I live?*

_____

_____

_____

_____

🙏 MY PRAYER TO GOD: Thank God for what you learned about Him. Ask God for His help to obey.

_____

_____

_____

Saturday | "Take Five" Weekly Review

Use the journal pages you filled out earlier this week to help you answer the questions below.

1. Use the space below to write out one of your favorite verses from your study this week. Why was this verse special to you?

_____

_____

_____

_____

_____

_____

2. What was your favorite truth about God that you learned this week?

_____

_____

_____

_____

_____

_____

3. How can you use what you learned about God this week to encourage someone else? *(Who will you tell about your great God? What will you tell them about Him?)*

_____

_____

_____

_____

_____

_____

4. What is one thing God taught you this past week that you want to change in order to be more like Him? Stop and ask God to give you the grace to obey!

_____

_____

_____

_____

_____

_____

5. How did "what you know about God" help you this past week? *(Think about a difficulty you faced or a decision you had to make where remembering the truth about God helped you do the right thing.)*

_____

_____

_____

_____

_____

_____

Psalm 95:6-7

Oh come, let us worship and bow down;
let us kneel before the LORD, our Maker!
For he is our God, and we are the people of
his pasture, and the sheep of his hand.

Sunday | Worship

You should worship God every day. But Sunday is a special day set aside in our week to really focus on giving worship to our great God. Use this sheet to help prepare your heart to worship the Lord at church today. Begin your "worship service" at home, praising God for who He is and what He has done for you.

God created you to worship Him.

Worthy are you, our Lord and God, to receive glory and honor and power, for you created all things, and by your will they existed and were created. (Revelation 4:11)

God is worthy of your worship.

Worthy is the Lamb who was slain, to receive power and wealth and wisdom and might and honor and glory and blessing! (Revelation 5:12)

The Psalm are all about our great God! Each chapter is full of incredible truths about God. Look back through this week's journal pages and write down at least 5 things you learned about our amazing God: "Who He is" or "What He does." Then take time to praise God, through prayer, for each thing you wrote down. You might even want to grab a hymnal and sing a song of praise to God.

I will praise Him for **Who He is**	I will praise Him for **What He does**
1. My God is: _____	1. My God does: _____
2. My God is: _____	2. My God does: _____
3. My God is: _____	3. My God does: _____
4. My God is: _____	4. My God does: _____
5. My God is: _____	5. My God does: _____

WEEK NINE

Psalm 100:3

Know that the LORD, he is God!
It is he who made us, and we are his;
we are his people, and the sheep of his pasture.

Monday | God is my... My God is...

PREPARE: Getting my heart ready to meet with God.

We need God's help to understand His Word. Begin your time in the Word today by thoughtfully praying these words of Scripture back to the Lord:

Give me understanding, that I may keep your law and observe it with my whole heart. (Psalm 119:34)

OBSERVE: Getting God's Word into my heart.

Read **Psalm 99:1-9** and seek to answer the question: *What do these verses teach me about My God?*

_____

_____

_____

_____

_____

APPLY: Getting God's Word into my life.

Think about what you learned about God. Ask: *If I really believe this truth about God, then how will I live?*

_____

_____

_____

_____

_____

MY PRAYER TO GOD: Thank God for what you learned about Him. Ask God for His help to obey.

_____

_____

_____

_____

Tuesday | God is my... My God is...

PREPARE: Getting my heart ready to meet with God.

We need God's help to understand His Word. Begin your time in the Word today by thoughtfully praying these words of Scripture back to the Lord:

> *Open my eyes, that I may behold wondrous things*
> *out of your law. (Psalm 119:18)*

OBSERVE: Getting God's Word into my heart.

Read **Psalm 100:1-5** and seek to answer the question: *What do these verses teach me about My God?*

_____

_____

_____

_____

APPLY: Getting God's Word into my life.

Think about what you learned about God. Ask: *If I really believe this truth about God, then how will I live?*

_____

_____

_____

_____

MY PRAYER TO GOD: Thank God for what you learned about Him. Ask God for His help to obey.

_____

_____

_____

_____

Wednesday | God is my... My God is...

⚔ PREPARE: Getting my heart ready to meet with God.

We need God's help to understand His Word. Begin your time in the Word today by thoughtfully praying these words of Scripture back to the Lord:

> You have said, "Seek my face." My heart says to you, "Your face, LORD, do I seek." (Psalm 27:8)

🔍 OBSERVE: Getting God's Word into my heart.

Read **Psalm 103:1-13** and seek to answer the question: *What do these verses teach me about My God?*

_____

_____

_____

_____

_____

⚓ APPLY: Getting God's Word into my life.

Think about what you learned about God. Ask: *If I really believe this truth about God, then how will I live?*

_____

_____

_____

_____

_____

⚔ MY PRAYER TO GOD: Thank God for what you learned about Him. Ask God for His help to obey.

_____

_____

_____

_____

Thursday | God is my... My God is...

PREPARE: Getting my heart ready to meet with God.

We need God's help to understand His Word. Begin your time in the Word today by thoughtfully praying these words of Scripture back to the Lord:

Make me to know your ways, O LORD; teach me your paths. Lead me in your truth and teach me, for you are the God of my salvation... (Psalm 25:4-5)

OBSERVE: Getting God's Word into my heart.

Read **Psalm 103:14-22** and seek to answer the question: *What do these verses teach me about My God?*

_____

_____

_____

_____

_____

APPLY: Getting God's Word into my life.

Think about what you learned about God. Ask: *If I really believe this truth about God, then how will I live?*

_____

_____

_____

_____

MY PRAYER TO GOD: Thank God for what you learned about Him. Ask God for His help to obey.

_____

_____

_____

_____

Friday | God is my... My God is...

PREPARE: Getting my heart ready to meet with God.

We need God's help to understand His Word. Begin your time in the Word today by thoughtfully praying these words of Scripture back to the Lord:

Teach me to do your will, for you are my God!
(Psalm 143:10a)

OBSERVE: Getting God's Word into my heart.

Read **Psalm 104:1-24** and seek to answer the question: *What do these verses teach me about My God?*

_____

_____

_____

_____

_____

APPLY: Getting God's Word into my life.

Think about what you learned about God. Ask: *If I really believe this truth about God, then how will I live?*

_____

_____

_____

_____

_____

MY PRAYER TO GOD: Thank God for what you learned about Him. Ask God for His help to obey.

_____

_____

_____

_____

Saturday | "Take Five" Weekly Review

Use the journal pages you filled out earlier this week to help you answer the questions below.

1. Use the space below to write out one of your favorite verses from your study this week. Why was this verse special to you?

_____

_____

_____

_____

_____

_____

2. What was your favorite truth about God that you learned this week?

_____

_____

_____

_____

_____

_____

3. How can you use what you learned about God this week to encourage someone else? *(Who will you tell about your great God? What will you tell them about Him?)*

_____

_____

_____

_____

_____

4. What is one thing God taught you this past week that you want to change in order to be more like Him? Stop and ask God to give you the grace to obey!

_____

_____

_____

_____

_____

_____

5. How did "what you know about God" help you this past week? *(Think about a difficulty you faced or a decision you had to make where remembering the truth about God helped you do the right thing.)*

_____

_____

_____

_____

_____

_____

Psalm 100:3

Know that the LORD, he is God!
It is he who made us, and we are his;
we are his people, and the sheep of his pasture.

Sunday | Worship

You should worship God every day. But Sunday is a special day set aside in our week to really focus on giving worship to our great God. Use this sheet to help prepare your heart to worship the Lord at church today. Begin your "worship service" at home, praising God for who He is and what He has done for you.

God created you to worship Him.

Worthy are you, our Lord and God, to receive glory and honor and power, for you created all things, and by your will they existed and were created. (Revelation 4:11)

God is worthy of your worship.

Worthy is the Lamb who was slain, to receive power and wealth and wisdom and might and honor and glory and blessing! (Revelation 5:12)

The Psalm are all about our great God! Each chapter is full of incredible truths about God. Look back through this week's journal pages and write down at least 5 things you learned about our amazing God: "Who He is" or "What He does." Then take time to praise God, through prayer, for each thing you wrote down. You might even want to grab a hymnal and sing a song of praise to God.

I will praise Him for **Who He is**	*I will praise Him for* **What He does**
1. My God is: _____	1. My God does: _____
2. My God is: _____	2. My God does: _____
3. My God is: _____	3. My God does: _____
4. My God is: _____	4. My God does: _____
5. My God is: _____	5. My God does: _____

WEEK TEN

Psalm 118:1

*Oh give thanks to the LORD, for he is good;
for his steadfast love endures forever!*

Monday | God is my... My God is...

PREPARE: Getting my heart ready to meet with God.

We need God's help to understand His Word. Begin your time in the Word today by thoughtfully praying these words of Scripture back to the Lord:

Give me understanding, that I may keep your law and observe it with my whole heart. (Psalm 119:34)

OBSERVE: Getting God's Word into my heart.

Read **Psalm 111-1-10** and seek to answer the question: *What do these verses teach me about My God?*

_____

_____

_____

_____

_____

APPLY: Getting God's Word into my life.

Think about what you learned about God. Ask: *If I really believe this truth about God, then how will I live?*

_____

_____

_____

_____

_____

MY PRAYER TO GOD: Thank God for what you learned about Him. Ask God for His help to obey.

_____

_____

_____

_____

Tuesday | God is my... My God is...

🙏 PREPARE: Getting my heart ready to meet with God.

We need God's help to understand His Word. Begin your time in the Word today by thoughtfully praying these words of Scripture back to the Lord:

Open my eyes, that I may behold wondrous things
out of your law. (Psalm 119:18)

🔍 OBSERVE: Getting God's Word into my heart.
Read **Psalm 113:1-9** and seek to answer the question: *What do these verses teach me about My God?*

_____

_____

_____

_____

_____

❓ APPLY: Getting God's Word into my life.
Think about what you learned about God. Ask: *If I really believe this truth about God, then how will I live?*

_____

_____

_____

_____

🙏 MY PRAYER TO GOD: Thank God for what you learned about Him. Ask God for His help to obey.

_____

_____

_____

_____

Wednesday | God is my... My God is...

PREPARE: Getting my heart ready to meet with God.

We need God's help to understand His Word. Begin your time in the Word today by thoughtfully praying these words of Scripture back to the Lord:

> You have said, "Seek my face." My heart says to you, "Your face, LORD, do I seek." (Psalm 27:8)

OBSERVE: Getting God's Word into my heart.

Read **Psalm 115:1-11** and seek to answer the question: *What do these verses teach me about My God?*

_____

_____

_____

_____

APPLY: Getting God's Word into my life.

Think about what you learned about God. Ask: *If I really believe this truth about God, then how will I live?*

_____

_____

_____

_____

MY PRAYER TO GOD: Thank God for what you learned about Him. Ask God for His help to obey.

_____

_____

_____

_____

PREPARE: Getting my heart ready to meet with God.

We need God's help to understand His Word. Begin your time in the Word today by thoughtfully praying these words of Scripture back to the Lord:

Make me to know your ways, O LORD; teach me your paths. Lead me in your truth and teach me, for you are the God of my salvation... (Psalm 25:4-5)

OBSERVE: Getting God's Word into my heart.
Read **Psalm 117:1-2** and seek to answer the question: *What do these verses teach me about My God?*

_____

_____

_____

_____

_____

APPLY: Getting God's Word into my life.
Think about what you learned about God. Ask: *If I really believe this truth about God, then how will I live?*

_____

_____

_____

_____

MY PRAYER TO GOD: Thank God for what you learned about Him. Ask God for His help to obey.

_____

_____

_____

_____

Friday | God is my... My God is...

🙏 PREPARE: Getting my heart ready to meet with God.

We need God's help to understand His Word. Begin your time in the Word today by thoughtfully praying these words of Scripture back to the Lord:

Teach me to do your will, for you are my God!
(Psalm 143:10a)

🔍 OBSERVE: Getting God's Word into my heart.

Read **Psalm 118:1-9, 14-16, 28-29** and seek to answer the question: *What do these verses teach me about My God?*

_____

_____

_____

_____

_____

🔱 APPLY: Getting God's Word into my life.

Think about what you learned about God. Ask: *If I really believe this truth about God, then how will I live?*

_____

_____

_____

_____

🙏 MY PRAYER TO GOD: Thank God for what you learned about Him. Ask God for His help to obey.

_____

_____

_____

_____

Saturday | "Take Five" Weekly Review

Use the journal pages you filled out earlier this week to help you answer the questions below.

1. Use the space below to write out one of your favorite verses from your study this week. Why was this verse special to you?

_____

_____

_____

_____

_____

2. What was your favorite truth about God that you learned this week?

_____

_____

_____

_____

_____

3. How can you use what you learned about God this week to encourage someone else? *(Who will you tell about your great God? What will you tell them about Him?)*

_____

_____

_____

_____

_____

4. What is one thing God taught you this past week that you want to change in order to be more like Him? Stop and ask God to give you the grace to obey!

_____

_____

_____

_____

_____

_____

5. How did "what you know about God" help you this past week? *(Think about a difficulty you faced or a decision you had to make where remembering the truth about God helped you do the right thing.)*

_____

_____

_____

_____

_____

_____

Psalm 118:1

Oh give thanks to the LORD, for he is good;
for his steadfast love endures forever!

Sunday | Worship

You should worship God every day. But Sunday is a special day set aside in our week to really focus on giving worship to our great God. Use this sheet to help prepare your heart to worship the Lord at church today. Begin your "worship service" at home, praising God for who He is and what He has done for you.

God created you to worship Him.

Worthy are you, our Lord and God, to receive glory and honor and power, for you created all things, and by your will they existed and were created. (Revelation 4:11)

God is worthy of your worship.

Worthy is the Lamb who was slain, to receive power and wealth and wisdom and might and honor and glory and blessing! (Revelation 5:12)

The Psalm are all about our great God! Each chapter is full of incredible truths about God. Look back through this week's journal pages and write down at least 5 things you learned about our amazing God: "Who He is" or "What He does." Then take time to praise God, through prayer, for each thing you wrote down. You might even want to grab a hymnal and sing a song of praise to God.

I will praise Him for **Who He is**	*I will praise Him for* **What He does**
1. My God is: _____	1. My God does: _____
2. My God is: _____	2. My God does: _____
3. My God is: _____	3. My God does: _____
4. My God is: _____	4. My God does: _____
5. My God is: _____	5. My God does: _____

WEEK ELEVEN

Psalm 130:3-4

If you, O LORD, should mark iniquities,
O Lord, who could stand?
But with you there is forgiveness,
that you may be feared.

Monday | God is my... My God is...

🙏 PREPARE: Getting my heart ready to meet with God.

We need God's help to understand His Word. Begin your time in the Word today by thoughtfully praying these words of Scripture back to the Lord:

Give me understanding, that I may keep your law and observe it with my whole heart. (Psalm 119:34)

🔍 OBSERVE: Getting God's Word into my heart.

Read **Psalm 121:1-8** and seek to answer the question: *What do these verses teach me about My God?*

_____

_____

_____

_____

_____

❓ APPLY: Getting God's Word into my life.

Think about what you learned about God. Ask: *If I really believe this truth about God, then how will I live?*

_____

_____

_____

_____

_____

🙏 MY PRAYER TO GOD: Thank God for what you learned about Him. Ask God for His help to obey.

_____

_____

_____

_____

Tuesday | God is my... My God is...

PREPARE: Getting my heart ready to meet with God.

We need God's help to understand His Word. Begin your time in the Word today by thoughtfully praying these words of Scripture back to the Lord:

Open my eyes, that I may behold wondrous things
out of your law. (Psalm 119:18)

OBSERVE: Getting God's Word into my heart.

Read **Psalm 130:1-8** and seek to answer the question: *What do these verses teach me about My God?*

_____

_____

_____

_____

APPLY: Getting God's Word into my life.

Think about what you learned about God. Ask: *If I really believe this truth about God, then how will I live?*

_____

_____

_____

_____

MY PRAYER TO GOD: Thank God for what you learned about Him. Ask God for His help to obey.

_____

_____

_____

_____

PREPARE: Getting my heart ready to meet with God.

We need God's help to understand His Word. Begin your time in the Word today by thoughtfully praying these words of Scripture back to the Lord:

> *You have said, "Seek my face." My heart says to you,*
> *"Your face, LORD, do I seek." (Psalm 27:8)*

OBSERVE: Getting God's Word into my heart.

Read **Psalm 135:3-14** and seek to answer the question: *What do these verses teach me about My God?*

_____

_____

_____

_____

_____

APPLY: Getting God's Word into my life.

Think about what you learned about God. Ask: *If I really believe this truth about God, then how will I live?*

_____

_____

_____

_____

_____

MY PRAYER TO GOD: Thank God for what you learned about Him. Ask God for His help to obey.

_____

_____

_____

_____

PREPARE: Getting my heart ready to meet with God.

We need God's help to understand His Word. Begin your time in the Word today by thoughtfully praying these words of Scripture back to the Lord:

Make me to know your ways, O LORD; teach me your paths. Lead me in your truth and teach me, for you are the God of my salvation... (Psalm 25:4-5)

OBSERVE: Getting God's Word into my heart.

Read **Psalm 136:1-9** and seek to answer the question: *What do these verses teach me about My God?*

_____

_____

_____

_____

_____

APPLY: Getting God's Word into my life.

Think about what you learned about God. Ask: *If I really believe this truth about God, then how will I live?*

_____

_____

_____

_____

MY PRAYER TO GOD: Thank God for what you learned about Him. Ask God for His help to obey.

_____

_____

_____

_____

Friday | God is my... My God is...

🙏 PREPARE: Getting my heart ready to meet with God.

We need God's help to understand His Word. Begin your time in the Word today by thoughtfully praying these words of Scripture back to the Lord:

Teach me to do your will, for you are my God!
(Psalm 143:10a)

🔍 OBSERVE: Getting God's Word into my heart.

Read **Psalm 138:1–8** and seek to answer the question: *What do these verses teach me about My God?*

_____

_____

_____

_____

❓ APPLY: Getting God's Word into my life.

Think about what you learned about God. Ask: *If I really believe this truth about God, then how will I live?*

_____

_____

_____

_____

🙏 MY PRAYER TO GOD: Thank God for what you learned about Him. Ask God for His help to obey.

_____

_____

_____

_____

Saturday | "Take Five" Weekly Review

Use the journal pages you filled out earlier this week to help you answer the questions below.

1. Use the space below to write out one of your favorite verses from your study this week. Why was this verse special to you?

_____

_____

_____

_____

_____

_____

2. What was your favorite truth about God that you learned this week?

_____

_____

_____

_____

_____

_____

3. How can you use what you learned about God this week to encourage someone else? (*Who will you tell about your great God? What will you tell them about Him?*)

_____

_____

_____

_____

_____

4. What is one thing God taught you this past week that you want to change in order to be more like Him? Stop and ask God to give you the grace to obey!

_____

_____

_____

_____

_____

_____

5. How did "what you know about God" help you this past week? *(Think about a difficulty you faced or a decision you had to make where remembering the truth about God helped you do the right thing.)*

_____

_____

_____

_____

_____

_____

Psalm 130:3-4

If you, O LORD, should mark iniquities,
O Lord, who could stand?
But with you there is forgiveness,
that you may be feared.

Sunday | Worship

You should worship God every day. But Sunday is a special day set aside in our week to really focus on giving worship to our great God. Use this sheet to help prepare your heart to worship the Lord at church today. Begin your "worship service" at home, praising God for who He is and what He has done for you.

God created you to worship Him.

Worthy are you, our Lord and God, to receive glory and honor and power, for you created all things, and by your will they existed and were created. (Revelation 4:11)

God is worthy of your worship.

Worthy is the Lamb who was slain, to receive power and wealth and wisdom and might and honor and glory and blessing! (Revelation 5:12)

The Psalm are all about our great God! Each chapter is full of incredible truths about God. Look back through this week's journal pages and write down at least 5 things you learned about our amazing God: "Who He is" or "What He does." Then take time to praise God, through prayer, for each thing you wrote down. You might even want to grab a hymnal and sing a song of praise to God.

I will praise Him for **Who He is**	*I will praise Him for* **What He does**
1. My God is: _____	1. My God does: _____
2. My God is: _____	2. My God does: _____
3. My God is: _____	3. My God does: _____
4. My God is: _____	4. My God does: _____
5. My God is: _____	5. My God does: _____

WEEK TWELVE

Psalm 145:3

*Great is the LORD, and greatly to be praised,
and his greatness is unsearchable.*

Monday | God is my... My God is...

🙏 PREPARE: Getting my heart ready to meet with God.

We need God's help to understand His Word. Begin your time in the Word today by thoughtfully praying these words of Scripture back to the Lord:

Give me understanding, that I may keep your law and observe it with my whole heart. (Psalm 119:34)

🔍 OBSERVE: Getting God's Word into my heart.

Read **Psalm 139:1–16** and seek to answer the question: *What do these verses teach me about My God?*

_____

_____

_____

_____

_____

❓ APPLY: Getting God's Word into my life.

Think about what you learned about God. Ask: *If I really believe this truth about God, then how will I live?*

_____

_____

_____

_____

🙏 MY PRAYER TO GOD: Thank God for what you learned about Him. Ask God for His help to obey.

_____

_____

_____

_____

Tuesday | God is my... My God is...

PREPARE: Getting my heart ready to meet with God.

We need God's help to understand His Word. Begin your time in the Word today by thoughtfully praying these words of Scripture back to the Lord:

> *Open my eyes, that I may behold wondrous things out of your law. (Psalm 119:18)*

OBSERVE: Getting God's Word into my heart.

Read **Psalm 145:1-9** and seek to answer the question: *What do these verses teach me about My God?*

_____

_____

_____

_____

APPLY: Getting God's Word into my life.

Think about what you learned about God. Ask: *If I really believe this truth about God, then how will I live?*

_____

_____

_____

_____

MY PRAYER TO GOD: Thank God for what you learned about Him. Ask God for His help to obey.

_____

_____

_____

_____

Wednesday | God is my... My God is...

PREPARE: Getting my heart ready to meet with God.

We need God's help to understand His Word. Begin your time in the Word today by thoughtfully praying these words of Scripture back to the Lord:

> *You have said, "Seek my face." My heart says to you,*
> *"Your face, LORD, do I seek." (Psalm 27:8)*

OBSERVE: Getting God's Word into my heart.

Read **Psalm 145:10-21** and seek to answer the question: *What do these verses teach me about My God?*

_____

_____

_____

_____

APPLY: Getting God's Word into my life.

Think about what you learned about God. Ask: *If I really believe this truth about God, then how will I live?*

_____

_____

_____

_____

MY PRAYER TO GOD: Thank God for what you learned about Him. Ask God for His help to obey.

_____

_____

_____

_____

Thursday | God is my... My God is...

🙏 PREPARE: Getting my heart ready to meet with God.

We need God's help to understand His Word. Begin your time in the Word today by thoughtfully praying these words of Scripture back to the Lord:

Make me to know your ways, O LORD; teach me your paths. Lead me in your truth and teach me, for you are the God of my salvation... (Psalm 25:4-5)

🔍 OBSERVE: Getting God's Word into my heart.

Read **Psalm 146:1-10** and seek to answer the question: *What do these verses teach me about My God?*

_____

_____

_____

_____

_____

❓ APPLY: Getting God's Word into my life.

Think about what you learned about God. Ask: *If I really believe this truth about God, then how will I live?*

_____

_____

_____

_____

🙏 MY PRAYER TO GOD: Thank God for what you learned about Him. Ask God for His help to obey.

_____

_____

_____

_____

Friday | God is my... My God is...

🙏 PREPARE: Getting my heart ready to meet with God.

We need God's help to understand His Word. Begin your time in the Word today by thoughtfully praying these words of Scripture back to the Lord:

> *Teach me to do your will, for you are my God!*
> *(Psalm 143:10a)*

🔍 OBSERVE: Getting God's Word into my heart.

Read **Psalm 147:1-11** and seek to answer the question: *What do these verses teach me about My God?*

_____

_____

_____

_____

⚓ APPLY: Getting God's Word into my life.

Think about what you learned about God. Ask: *If I really believe this truth about God, then how will I live?*

_____

_____

_____

_____

🙏 MY PRAYER TO GOD: Thank God for what you learned about Him. Ask God for His help to obey.

_____

_____

_____

_____

Saturday | "Take Five" Weekly Review

Use the journal pages you filled out earlier this week to help
you answer the questions below.

1. Use the space below to write out one of your favorite verses
   from your study this week. Why was this verse special to
   you?

---

2. What was your favorite truth about God that you learned
   this week?

---

3. How can you use what you learned about God this week to
   encourage someone else? *(Who will you tell about your great
   God? What will you tell them about Him?)*

---

4. What is one thing God taught you this past week that you want to change in order to be more like Him? Stop and ask God to give you the grace to obey!

_____

_____

_____

_____

_____

_____

5. How did "what you know about God" help you this past week? *(Think about a difficulty you faced or a decision you had to make where remembering the truth about God helped you do the right thing.)*

_____

_____

_____

_____

_____

_____

Psalm 145:3

Great is the Lord, and greatly to be praised,
and his greatness is unsearchable.

Sunday | Worship

You should worship God every day. But Sunday is a special day set aside in our week to really focus on giving worship to our great God. Use this sheet to help prepare your heart to worship the Lord at church today. Begin your "worship service" at home, praising God for who He is and what He has done for you.

God created you to worship Him.

Worthy are you, our Lord and God, to receive glory and honor and power, for you created all things, and by your will they existed and were created. (Revelation 4:11)

God is worthy of your worship.

Worthy is the Lamb who was slain, to receive power and wealth and wisdom and might and honor and glory and blessing! (Revelation 5:12)

The Psalm are all about our great God! Each chapter is full of incredible truths about God. Look back through this week's journal pages and write down at least 5 things you learned about our amazing God: "Who He is" or "What He does." Then take time to praise God, through prayer, for each thing you wrote down. You might even want to grab a hymnal and sing a song of praise to God.

I will praise Him for **Who He is**	*I will praise Him for* **What He does**
1. My God is: _____	1. My God does: _____
2. My God is: _____	2. My God does: _____
3. My God is: _____	3. My God does: _____
4. My God is: _____	4. My God does: _____
5. My God is: _____	5. My God does: _____

Made in the USA
Coppell, TX
26 March 2025

47553750R00075